PROPHETIC KINGDOM

Poetry with a Purpose

Patricia Dorsey

Published by:

EMPOWER ME BOOKS, INC.

A Subsidiary of Empower Me Enterprises, Inc.
P.O. Box 16153 Durham, North Carolina 27704
www.EmpowerMeBooks.com

ISBN: 978-1732773127
Printed In the United States of America

PROPHETIC KINGDOM

Poetry with a Purpose

~ The **poetry** within this book was written with special intensity that portrays the expression of feelings and ideas by the use of distinctive styles and rhythm.

In this book, you will also be introduced to *prose* written throughout this artistic peace, as a technique of language that exhibits more of a natural flow of speech, grammatical structure or free form, which will not always use rhythm or rhyme. ~

Acknowledgements

First and foremost, I give praise and adoration to the Most High God, Jesus Christ my Lord and Savior, for the gift in poetry.

I would like to thank my Son, James Franklin, for always being one of my biggest supporters. I would like to thank God for using Empower Me Books, Inc. to help me birth this book. I would like to thank my Mom and my Aunts for inspiring me through their own poetry from a very young age. I would like to acknowledge myself for rising to the occasion to complete the task that God laid on my heart, even when I wanted to give-up! Thank you to everyone who, prayed, congratulated or pushed me on this journey.

Thank you last but certainly not least for my Church Family, One Love Christian Church for their continued support and prayers.

To My Poetically Inspired Readers:

I have penned this book as a way to evangelize, to inspire, to encourage and to embrace a specific subgroup of peculiar people who are hurting. I hope that the words written in this book will sooth with loving words that nourish, impel and inspire. I have been granted this spiritual baby which has brought forth new vision and which has allowed me to write this prose and poetry after recovering from surgery. God allowed me to relieve stress through written expression as a way to also encourage myself. These words have been prophetically inspired.

Many thanks and Love!

Patricia Dorsey

Poetically Inspired Contents

❖ **Section 1**   11
Poems and Prose about God

❖ **Section 2**   20
Poems and Prose for Prayer, Love,
Inspiration & Encouragement

❖ **Section 3**   29
Poems and Prose for Mothers and
Women

❖ **Section 4**   36
Poems and Prose for Crisis in Faith

❖ **Section 5**   44
Poems and Prose about Life, Abuse &
Rejection

❖ **Section 6**   58
Prose - Poetry for Loss & Grief

❖ **Section 7**   61
Poems and Prose for Black Women &
Discrimination

About the Author   71

❖ Section 1

Poems and Prose
about God

The Book

The book is real, if you read it.
It's the book that tells us that Jesus lives again!
The words that were left for us to see,
That in some that read it, they too shall believe.

This is the book that God gave us to believe,
To know that Jesus would come again.
He knew who would believe.

This book that disciples and holy men of old wrote and spoke,
Was left to us as a gift to follow, with instructions and Jesus's quotes.
You see, if you read this book and you believe,
Then this book called God's Holy word,
Will come to life and set you free.
And you will see that this bible has predicted everything right.

Jesus the Messiah

Jesus, Jesus, the man called Messiah.
The Son of God, who was called to lead many to follow.
He was the healer and deliverer.
The supernatural miracle worker.
He walked on water like no other;
He could raise the dead and increase the bread.
He came to save the world although some mocked and laughed
And even scolded him with contempt;
But Jesus praised God with his lips.

John the Baptist warned others that a Messiah was coming.
The one who was the light of the world that would lead many from their sins.

This Messiah, they crucified.
They hung him, the hung him high.
They nailed his hands to the cross;
But with the shedding of blood, it saved the world of its awful sins,
If they only knew that Jesus died to replace the wicked world of sin.
They killed the King of kings,
Only to find that he would be risen from his grave,
To live again, to give us eternal life to live through his name.

Jesus is real

Jesus is real.
If you believe,
He came to die for you and me.
He came to save the world from their sin.
With so much drama with one another,
So much hate, so much sorrow and so much hurting of others.
He came so that we may live again.

Now you see the bible and its instruction was here for us to live by,
Not to be condemned by.
But Jesus died and came back again,
To let the world know, that they could live again.
If you believe in your heart that Jesus died on the cross to save the
world from its sin,
Then you will be saved and live again.
To see the Kingdom of Heaven as you stand.

God is Real Can't You See

God is real, can you see that he made this world for you and me.
He gave us life to live again.
He formed the world in seven days.
Can you see the birds in the air?
Can you see the grass that's green?
Can you see the food that he made?
Thousands of fruit and vegetables that you cannot even name,
He made the tree so you could enjoy this very specific history.

But how can you not see this brilliant God;
So understanding and kind hearted,
With so much compassion and love for us?
You can see God in all that he has demonstrated in this world.
You can see all the things that he made for you and for me;
He gave us gifts to complete this foundation to live in Peace.

Can't you see me?
Says God, to those who say "There is no God".
Can't you see me in the wind when it blows?
Can you not feel the presence of wind when it blows?
You can feel the presence of the wind when it blows,
But you don't know where it comes from.
Can't you see me in the sun; the stars in the sky?
Can't you see me in the trees and in the birds and the bees?
Can't you see me in the Newborn child when it's born from its
mother's womb?

I knew you before you were born.
I had a plan and a purpose for you;
But it is up to you to decide to follow the right path.
If you decide to follow the evil ways of the world,
You will be lead to destruction for sure.
Now if you decide to follow me, God the creator and my instructions
And commandments,

Then you will be surely to have a good and prosperous life;
With peace, joy and love.
Surely, you will have eternal life.

The Creator

I am the one who created the whole universe.
The one who makes the sunshine everyday upon the earth.
It is God that you should believe.

God said, "I am that I am".
In essence, all that you need, "I am that I am".

The one and only who is real.
Every day, every night of your life.
It hurts God's heart indeed,
To see those whom he love in need.
And knowing all,
God wonders why.
Why they never call on him!

God says, "If they just ask I can satisfy them with their needs".
God says, "I will give you everything".

Are You Ready?

God says, Are you ready; Are you without a doubt ready?
Are you ready to meet the Maker, the Creator,
And the Holy One, who loves you so much?
I know all that is going on.
I did not give you the world, to tear it apart.
I gave you all everything you see; and still some of you don't believe.

Just remember,
Before your time,
There was a generation that did not make it to the promise land.
They saw the signs of God like never before;
But, when they were free,
They pretended there was no God that could see.
They worshipped things that they should not have.
Moses tried to help them go over into the promise land.
Well as the word says,
Only their children made it to the Promise Land.

Oh and guess what,
That was you and me!
With this world we have everything we love.
He gave us more than what we could afford.
Look around, can't you see, we have all the food we can eat. We
have a beautiful earth to breath fresh air.
I have gifts that God gave us to build this world for sure. The talents
and the gifts that we have, God put those in our head.

He gave us so much more;
Why?
So we could be comfortable, but God also wanted you to see the
creation that was given to man to be fulfilled.

Now don't think all this stuff in the world just came by itself,
without anyone.

I have better things for you. You see, in the next world that will be
built again;
But I love you all so much that I am even going to give you eternal
life to live again free from all pain, hurt, sorrow; but instead, LOVE!

God says, Are you ready?
Do you know the Maker, the one who is our Creator?
Are you ready to meet the maker; the one who perfects you and
made you?
Are you ready, to be born again; this is more than success;
More than health;
More than religion;
More than responsibility;
And more than Life.

Yes a beautiful life is to be expected; no more sorrow, no more pain;
No more death, no more sickness, no more affliction;
No more addiction, no more hate, and no more heart breaks;
No more strife, no more lies, no more tears from your eyes.
No more killing, no more killing, no more hurting people freely.
No more envy, no more jealousy, no more robbing others of joy;
No more sickness, no more disease,
For the body God gave us is external,
So be thankful for the New Life that God has prepared for both you
and me.

Thou Kingdom come, God's will be done, on earth as it is in Heaven.

❖ Section 2

Poems and Prose
for Prayer, Love,
Inspiration &
Encouragement

Prayer for Inspiration in Life

Sometimes in life Lord, people may feel like they don't know which way to go. They may feel like they are going on a narrow road. Sometimes they may feel like life is so hard, but we put our trust in you, the God above. Life can be sometimes be filled with ups and downs, God can move the inner secrets of our heart so we don't give up, that we may grow in grace and God you build our strength day by day. When we feel like life is about to knock us down, we give it to you God to turn it around.

Be Careful

People of Color young and old,
    Be careful out here in this world of old.
This world is filled with so much hate that it makes you
wonder what is going to happen next.

    So much crime, so many bad things that you hate to see
    every time you turn on the TV.

Someone killed, someone raped, someone robbed and so much
more.
    It makes you wonder if the people who do such things
    have a conscience.
Do they feel bad for the things that they have done?
    They know that there is a God above, who sees everything
    that's going on.

Some say,
    There is no God anywhere.
Do they really know that, when they arose in the morning that
it was God's Mercy for them to breathe?
    The fresh air that God gave them to live again, he loves us
    so, in spite of what we done.
He sees the bad in this world, but I believe he's waiting on us.
    We need to change our evil ways, because the people who
    do such things, will not get away with it.
One day it is going to be too late and they are going to wish
that they had stayed.

    Time is running out for this evil world.
It's time to repent, to stop our wicked ways and it's time to
change our hearts.
    You see God loves for us is so strong. If we change our
    ways and follow Gods laws and obey his word. God will
    give you external.

Life: God gave us all we need in this world for sure in this world things you just can't name for us to enjoy.

One big day in this world, if you live right God will give you more for your life you see when you leave this world, with your spirit gone life has just began.

You will be amazed at what the next life have for us,

If you continue in your evil way your soul will be lost forever and forever again that is this story.

God has a plan for you and me to live again in a beautiful paradise.

Prayer: Lord I Need You

Lord I was just thinking about all the things that I go through. I know that I need to have faith. I know that you are there. But sometimes, it feels like a heavy load, like I cannot go on. It's like walking up a hill, and it seems like you are never there; but I know that if I put my trust in you, you are there with your arms opened wide. Reminding me that you are a loving God that wants his child to learn and live. You remind me that when I am in need, you are my help to move on. God you see me and I know that you are a loving God. You have carried me along, carried my load. You build my faith and trust in you all the more.

Amen

There is a Season

There is a season for everything. It came to me one day in the spirit that we as individuals have people that come in like friends, job opportunities and more and we think that without a doubt they are meant to last for life. Ecclesiastes 3: 1-11, teaches that to everything, there is a season for every activity, but God does want us to know that our friends, our jobs, our relationship with people, will not always last. So don't get discouraged when these things are not available. New things will overcome old things. Sometimes we think those old things are meant to be forever, but some things are just not meant to be. Better things will come.

Abraham and Sarah

Let me tell you the story of Abraham and Sarah.
    They had favor with God, like no others.
You see Abraham was truly a man of God that followed God often.
    God told Abraham that he would be the father of a son and be a
    father of many nations although he was approaching the age of
    one hundred.
Abraham thought it was impossible.
    His wife was also in old age, she just laughed and said there could
    be no way.
This must be a joke, and the wife went on to say, why not just take the
maid.
    The maid gave up a son, little did Abraham know that his trouble
    had just begun.

Sometimes in life we have to learn not to be so impatient,
    When God tells us what he has purposed and stop trying to fix it.
God came through anyway to tell them of their mistake.
    God sent to angels to warn them before it became too late.
Trust God Abraham, you will be a father of many nations.
    Now due to the side issues now occurring with the maid,
Old Sarah sent her away.

    What they did was trouble, and this story teaches us something.
If Abraham had only but stood on the promises of God with all of his
heart he would have never had maid troubles.
    Abraham still became the father of many nations.
That today could include both me and you.

Look Around You!

Look around you, what do you see?
>A world that has Change from the things in the world, which we once enjoyed every day has gone away.

All the activity, all the entertainment, all the public events, they typical day to day.
>All the shopping and manufacturing

Look there is more to say,
>Look around you, what do you think?

Is the world coming to an end or is this just a fling;
>Or maybe it's time for a change.

We could use a much better world to live in.
>Or is it the almighty God's anger and wrath from sin that has caused these things that we are seeing.

He's patient with us every day of our life, even with all the strife.
>We are so unthankful for all the things in the world that he has done for us.

Some don't like the way they were made,
>After being created in His image.

And still others may even complain about all the food that He made.
>Then some who claim to be called by His name,

Fight among each other with all types of religious games and division.
>I wonder do they even know the true God up yonder!

If the people who are called by my name would walk in love, obey and worship me.
>Not the things of the world, then they would see,

How wonderful it is to hear plainly and with such clarity.

Prayers are Powerful

When you pray if you only believe it in your heart just the same as in your spoken word, prayers can heal, prayers can save, prayers can take your worries away. If you believe it in your heart and confess it with your mouth, then the power of prayer will come to life. You will see the power of prayer is so strong that it will send away all the evil when you speak the word. Therefore, keep praying and believing and your prayers will be revealed.

The Plans

Eyes have not seen, nor have ears heard, the things, the plans, that God has for us to see. The plans, the life, the beautiful, brilliant things that he has prepared for you and me, have not entered into the heart of man. The things, a new life, to live again offered to those who trust and believe in the plan of Jesus and to see the heavenly things in which God has prepared.

When I Call on Jesus Prayer Poem

When I call on Jesus,
    All things are possible.
When I call on Jesus, He hears me.
    He hears me in my sorrow.
When I call on Jesus there is Power in his name, the name of Jesus all
around us.
    Trust Jesus,
Even when you don't see him.
    His spirit he sent us in the Holy Spirit,
Along with his written word gives so much power;
    In his name, even the enemy tremors and cowers.

Keep giving Jesus glory,
    Keep lifting up his name to heaven!
The name of Jesus is so powerful, that we can truly feel His presence
all around us.

    -Amen-

❖ **Section 3**

**Poems and Prose
for Mothers and
Women**

The Phenomenal Woman with a Purpose

A phenomenal woman I am to be,

With a purpose in my life, I am extraordinary,

I'm an astonishing woman,

And sensational in what I need;

Stunning and marvelous when I want to be.

An Independent phenomenal when I want to be,

I live life to be spectacular, incredible and amazing.

When I walk in my purpose to be, you'll see,

That when you have faith and trust God,

For what you desire, it will happen miraculously.

What a wonderful, blessing from above,

God is so tremendous and unbelievable you see;

He has a story for you and for me.

The life of a virtuous woman he has given me,

He will make a way for your life and more,

He knows you, for who you are,

Because he searches your heart deep.

Phenomenal woman be strong,

Know that God has carried you all along.

Woman to Woman

Dear I just wanted to say rather you receive this message or not I'm going to say it anyway. We as woman need to have more, pride, with ourselves to be a virtuous woman, and not to be taken lightly by the man folks of today.

I wish when I was young that I was wise enough, to be a leader and not follow the crowd. It would have been nice to know how to carry myself in an elegant way, because when a guy really likes you, he will wait.

When I was young I got pregnant at 16 years old; there was never someone to teach me the right way until after the fall. They waited until I got pregnant to tell me about the birds and the bees, and I was like what?

I was searching for a Love that could give me peace in the mist of the storm, a love that would meet my need;

Then I found the love of God to fulfil that need. He may not give you what you want, but he meets the need right where you are and is always on time when you need him.

You guessed it right, his name is Jesus.

He's Jesus the Prince of Peace, God or God
Almighty my first love, a God whom never takes
flight.

And yes there was a time when I didn't know how
I was going to make it, but God showed up right
on time, it was the very time that I needed.

He's made a way out of some way,
He sent someone to find favor on me.

II

Woman to woman
Have you ever been in love then you will know
how I feel. Most women dream of that favorite
type of man in this life coming to rescue them, but
have you really, really been in love true love with
the type of men that you know without a double
that he is the one?
The one that was there when you didn't have no
one else to go to; he was there to comfort you, love
you and hold you.
I just wanted to say all that is good, but I just want
to let you know that true love, love that's there
when you call on it is likened to God's love.

III

Woman to woman
Have you ever been abused, confused, hurt and

refused?
Then you know if you've ever been down that
road with someone you thought was true but later
found that they did everything in their heart to
keep you confused.
They manipulated you as much as they could, to
make you feel like you was nothing to them but a
fool.

IV

Woman to woman
I have a word for you, be strong and bold, and get
up and go. Look at yourself and say hey you, I am
somebody, and I refuse to be used, and abuse and
manipulated by anybody.
I am going to pick myself up and be strong,
I am not going down, but I am going up and I am
a smart black and beautiful woman. And, you
know what I am going to do to help somebody,
somebody who was just like me, that was weak
and hurting, In need of a freeing.

I deserve to do this one thing. I can step away
from anything.
If there is somebody out there who been through
hell just like me,
I am going to encourage, and allow these word to
be nourishment to help them in need,

To know that they can do it!
If God did it for me, he can do it for them and set
them free,

Free from this mess they are in. Make them strong and delivered to be that bold woman they should be.

A Mother's Love

The life God allowed me to birth through you,
Was so amazing, it left me praising God alone for you.
I was so astonished with joy,
Love and amazement,
When I had you.
It was like the healing power of joy,
Just to hear your first cry.
When you came into this world,
I held you, it was love at first sight.
I never knew life could be so beautiful
When my first born came into sight.
He came into this world, a blessing,
A cherishment and testament of my pure love
With a future so bright.
Love them, cherish them, and care for them;
Protect them from the dangers of the world;
That was the plight.
I'll always pray that Gods hand is always around you;
To keep you safe forever more.

❖ Section 4

Poems and
Prose for Crisis
in Faith

God, God where are you?

The world says, God, God where are
you?
And what do I say?
My response is:
I gave you this world with everything,
That included the Ten -
Commandments that you refuse to
obey.
I gave you the sun in the sky, to rise
and brighten up your day.

I gave you everything from A – Z, so
many things I gave you in life, so that
you could live to build a beautiful
world of things.
Every bad thing in this world you all
did it to yourself.
I see the evil in this world created by
man; all the crime, hurt, pain jealousy
hate, the hurting of the innocent.
You even manipulate each other for
money and you disobey your mother.

He gave you 10 rules to follow,
But you refused and don't even bother.
Now the world has so much evil that
man created among one another,
That he world is out of control and
very much out of order.

The greed and selfishness, the coldness
shown to each other,
There is no love to help one another.
There is fear and control used to bring
about disorder,
But God is the ORDER.

There is a greater one you will soon
see,
One that has the power to move all
these things.
Now that the world is going crazy,
The one who died for your sins
Will very soon step in.
He will drive away the evil,
So don't fear what is going on.
What's coming next, is going to be
extraordinarily great,
Just get ready, don't be late.
Because he's coming quickly,
You'll look up and he's there just like
that.

God Do You Hear Me?

God says I hear your cries and I feel
your pain.
I see your tears even when you wipe
them away.
I hear your prayers, even late in the
night.

Don't think that I don't care.
I see the world with people who are
rebellious by my sight.
I gave them my son who they killed. I
sent the first generation all of my love,
That they may live.

They saw my signs and wonder from
heaven above,
But they turn to worship evil and more,
so I decided to wait and give the world
another chance;
To live eternally.

One day there will be no more sorrow,
no pain, no killing, no evil and your
tears will be wiped away.

So I am coming soon to destroy all
wicked things,
So let your tears be gone.

The time is near so get ready for sure,
for I will come so fast, you will open
your eyes and see me above.

Lord Why Me

Being a Christian is not easy at all,
because you go through trials and
tribulations;
But guess what?
In the middle of all the consequences, it
was worth it all.
Having been lied on and talked about
after much kindness and love had been
shown to those around, only to be
unfortunate in finding the return of
what was given.

I go to church,
To assemble myself together with other
Christian Saints,
But the Devil is there doing his work
also.
Surprise!
Children of God can also be so rude,
cruel and self-centered.
They are without fear of God.
All in all,
I learned for myself to be committed to
the Lord.
I learned to love myself and to depend
on the Almighty Lord above.

The reason I came to God because I
was too letting the Devil use me.
Much hate, lies, sorrow,

I was engaging in it all. Most of all,
I wanted God's peace, God's Love and
God's divine attention.
I wanted to be used as the example of a
true committed Christian.
I learned this one thing,
Jesus loves me regardless of what I've
done, or what I was.

I had learned Jesus for myself.
I had to love.
Those who lied on me, tried to use me,
I now show love to those who were my
enemy.
Most of all,
Jesus loves me regardless of what I've
done, or what I was.
He has shown me how to love without
being a Judge.

We Have Lost Our Touch

We as a people have really lost touch with
ourselves and with others as well.
I'm not going to butter coat anything.
In my opinion, we are living in the last day, it
seems.

As the Bible says, in 2nd Timothy 3 and 1 says
some things.
"In the last days perilous times shall come. For
men shall be lovers of their own selves,
covetous, boasters, proud, blasphemers,
disobedient to parents, unthankful, unholy…"
This verse signifies, how we as a people are
concerned with only ourselves, we have so
much pride.

All this self-satisfaction, bragging, and
coveting what other people have, with an evil
desire inside.

Have we no shame,
We wake up every day.
Blessed to see the sunshine and golden rays.
Birds sing of the coming light of a new day.
Surrounding us is a roof over our heads,
Food on our table to eat.
We have made it

Some are still unthankful to God and as people
do not realize the blessings that we have, that

could be taken away just like that!
They pretend to have no fear, and pretend that
there is no God,
But inside they are well aware of one that
created all.

❖ **Section 5**

Poems and Prose about Life, Abuse & Rejection

You Don't Know My Story

If you knew my story would you judge me?
Or would you see me as the person you thought you knew for sure!
Yes I smile and I seem happy most of the time and sometimes I'll
welcome you with a smile and a warm hug will be applied.
Inside sometimes I used to hurt from the pain that was took for
granted long ago by someone that broke my heart by people
especially those who I never despised or envied.
But I kept my faith with the Lord's strength because of the grace of
God and his great gratitude and his mercy and kind, that kept me
with the smile spontaneously made me strong on the inside. My
story is to say God Loves us so much that he will never leave nor
forsake us, even when we are alone.
There were times that I felt God was so far away and I thought that
he did not hear my prayers as I prayed each day.
Even after it all, having been lied on and mocked, when they see my
face I smile. They wonder why they have not succeeded at braking
me down.
I look at them with a cheerful smile, because they realized that they
could never really break me down.
All because I serve the higher one with the crown.

You don't know my story,
Or would you rather be in my shoes.
When I was young I didn't know what to do.
My dad was gone by the time I was 5, and all I knew was that he
was moving out of town.
I asked my mom where my dad was,
She just looked at me and shook her head.
We moved on to a new place,

With my 5 sisters and 1 brother, my mom endured the race.
She raised us as best as she could,
As we encountered the struggle we soon knew how to learn things
on our own.
My mom never had much time for us,
And I always felt rejected.
When I found God, I cried
And he wiped the tears from my eyes that I tried to hide.
God made me strong,
All the hurt and pain and rejection I felt was gone.
Then I realized all this time, that I thought I could not survive,
God had helped me realize how I could thrive.
God had a plan and had me in His strong right hand,
Just to give me faith and peace, I had to just trust to see.
God's purpose and plan for me never changed in life,
Through all the ups and downs God made me strong;
But my rejection didn't end when I was young.
I suppose it went on for quite a while,
But my trials made me strong!

Abuse

Have you ever been abused and hurt?
Taken advantage of by someone you hated.

Standing around others with a smile on your face,
Does that look okay?

The inside of you is hurting with pain and hurt that you regret for
the very rest of your life.

You wished that you weren't here,
But under the circumstance that enhanced stimulation that
cultivated the situation happened over time.
In my mind,
I just cried,
Feeling bad just about all of the time.

I was abused at the hands of someone and misused by them
repeatedly
By nothing caused or deserved by me.

Treated like I was nothing,
Except someone they could manipulate, handle and control;
Having no morals, no love at all.

I felt so misused and empty on the inside.
I just wanted to scream out loud and make it all go away.
Deep inside I had the courage to depart and go, it was my best
effort to stop this crime.

So I left, now free to help someone else escape this same crime.
I've decide to be free, not to use others or to manipulate.
If you too were lied too,
Have courage, get help!
Don't continue to let them hurt you.

Have faith,
Leave and get help!
Let's stop this mess and get us some justice.
Expose this evil spirit for all it is,
So you can be free from the cycle of abuse.

Life

Ever felt like Life was knocking you down;
Left you wondering why there was no love around.
I've been lied on, talked about, setup and traps were even laid
By people who disliked or envied me.

Through all the envying, jealousness, hate and sorrow that may be
thrown at you due to people's foolish ways, God will deal with them
in his very own way.
Sometimes they want to be like you; they see you, they see your
good heart and may attempt to destroy you; so be careful in what
you lay your trust.
The devil comes to steal, kill and destroy.
Believe me, these are the things that he guarantees.

You see I had to learn not to be like them.
I learned that the greater one lives down on the inside of me.

It's not about what you have or don't have,
Don't you see?
Because what God has planned for you and for me,
Is much greater than what your very eyes may see.
No matter how much people talk and hate on you or me,
It will only make you stronger to manage,
Oh you just wait and see.

Sometime life can be very hard,
We all have our ups and downs.
But life is sweet you see,
By the Grace of God he's given thee.
He will carry your burden and heal your wounded heart;
For real,
Just you wait and see.

You must however,
Trust God with your external life,
And he will show you all things that will come to you in life,
All spiritually, physically, supernaturally,
Oh what a Life!

How You May Feel

Sometimes in life, we all go through pain and sometimes in life, we have so much hate and some have been used and abused. You may wonder why the person who is crude can get away with the things they have done to you.

It hurt you so bad, to feel betrayed.
Especially by someone who never thought would treat you that way; but, somehow you found, the time to try to forget about the bad times.

You want to run back into the same, hurt and pain. You pray to God, "Why me?" "Why is this happening to me?" "What have I done to have deserved this pain?"
"Please hear me God, please take it away."

But you pray and you pray and finally hear God say that you don't deserve the pain and hate and the crude things that come your way. He goes on to tell you, that he doesn't like what is happening in this world when Adam and Eve, open the door, but I did left the word for you so that you have power to overcome, these things.

Get up! Be strong!
Get away from the Devil. Don't continue to be around, this evil. Leave! You have the strength to go! Don't let the enemy keep pulling you down the hole. There is help for you, don't you see?
I gave all this talent for men to use on your journey; to help those who need this word so that they can be set free.

Rejection

How many of you have ever felt rejected in life? Rejection is a spirit.
It preys and causes you to feel worthless and unwanted.
Have you ever felt rejected? When you try so hard desperately to
give them all your love and each time you naturally give and do
everything in your desire to love them, they refuse to show love back
to you.

Rejection can come in many ways to make you feel worthless and
unwanted. To make you have self-pity but you have to overcome
this spirit. Abandonment, loneliness and deep pain inside will make
you feel unwanted in many ways.

Strong woman, strong man,
That rejection has beat you down and made you feel this way.
Rise up and get to know the Spirit filled God and pray.
Accept the fact that until you get it deep down in your spirit and
veins,
That you are accepted, loved and appreciated by the God above.
You don't need or even have to settle for very person that comes
along.

You have to heal your soul and your mind before you compromise
or accommodate any relationship less it fall.
Don't compromise at all, because you feel the need to be loved by
someone who will toss you to and fro and make you feel worthless
and useless.
No, don't settle at all.

Don't settle for those who reject you or accept you.
Instead learn to love on you.

-A Short Prayer for Rejection-
In the name of Jesus, I renounce every spirit of rejection. I renounce
the spirit of fear, I command the memory of any and all times I was

rejected by family, friends or my parents to come out of my memory. In Jesus name,

-Amen-

Keeping Negativity Away

When a spirit of negativity tries to come your way, seek God and pray.
Pray that your heart is guarded and garment your soul with praise.
Focus on God to give you strength to control the thoughts within your mind.

Speak prosperity and positivity in your life: pray and release the spirit of fear.

Be released from the negativity of the world, and from the disappointments and stress.

Ask the Lord to guide your thoughts in the direction of positivity.

Surround yourself with positive people and change your thought pattern of thinking.

Encourage yourself with confidence and be uplifted in peace and hope.

Cherish yourself with admiration, without the need of other people's approval.

Ask God to break away every stronghold in my life.

I pray that it is broken in Jesus Name,
-Amen!-

I Have Loved and Lost

I have loved and I have lost. I have even took their fault.
There was a time that I kept inside all the pain I felt. I was quiet as a
mouse.
Sometimes people got a way of pretending to be your friend or
whatever don't you see;
Laughing in your face and behind your back.
They speculate what they think.
They fabricate what they do know,
All they do is hate.
I just keep a smile on my face,
I know deep down inside,
That will give me the peace I need to survive just fine.
All the times that people wanted me to fall,
God was there to catch me through it all.
He keeps me in line.

Looking for Love

It's not easy when you are looking for love in all the wrong places,
yeah!
You see,
It all begins when you are hurt, abused, broken hearted or misused.
Sometimes you may not have felt love when you were small. It
doesn't matter if you are a boy or girl.
You see,
Love is something that makes the world go round.
You search high and low for someone you trust;
Then you find out about their betrayal of trust.

So finally,
This is what usually happens when a heart is broken...
Instead of waiting for it to heal,
You rush to find love again and again.
You think it will take away the hurt and pain,
So then you are at it again.

This person took you for granted
And then dropped you like a ball, a hot potato or a bad habit.
Some were abused physically or mentally when they were young,
They carried the pain inside and told no one.
Only if they had reached out to someone they could trust,
Maybe it could have been dealt with and stopped.

Some are so afraid because they think it's their fault,
The person may have manipulated and lied to you,
All so that they could use and disrespect you,
They told you to tell no one or they could hurt you.

It is because of this you see,
That we as adults need to teach our children
About these types of things.
They need to know not to be afraid to tell you

About this senseless thing.
It could be your new boyfriend, or a neighbor you trust.
They pretend to be nice or even someone your family thought it could trust.

Okay,
It's like this,
Don't be afraid to tell someone.
If someone in your family doesn't believe you, tell a friend, tell a teacher,
Tell someone and BE BOLD!

Be strong and don't let them continue to use you.
They were wrong to do those things,
So tell someone right away.
If you don't the pain continues for someone else.
Don't let them get away, it was wrong, not right.
I dislike those type of people that take advantage of such precious life.

So BE BOLD, be strong and courageous,
Get ready to get that evil away from you forever!
-Trust in God-

❖ **Section 6**

Prose - Poetry
about Loss & Grief

Poetry for Loss and Grief

I know you missed them when they went away,
But God had to take them because they could not
endure the pain if they stayed.
The pain was deep, the pain was intense and that
made them feel like there was no hope.
With the hope of God, it gave them faith to hold on
just a little while longer;
But when the love of God came and took the pain
away,
It sure was love he gave on that day.

All the pain, all the hate, sorrow and more was gone,
All they could feel was his love, with the presence of
God's love was a spiritual moment they may not
have been able to explain,
But the inner spirit inside, it felt no pain and to say
and be a servant to God it was time to be a part of
God's plan.

God said don't worry about your loved one. He will
watch over them, and they are safe in his arms.
You will weep and there will be grief because of the
loss, you will miss,
But weeping may endure for a moment but joy
cometh in the morning as read in Psalm 30:5.

You will sometime grieve when you think of them,
Or when you remember the love you shared always
with open hands.
One day you all will meet in heaven one day,

When that special day comes, just be ready when it's
your time to enter this beautiful heavenly paradise
place.
I hope this poem speaks to your heart,
If you have not received salvation today, you can
receive Jesus today.

In a very special way, make this your very own day,
By giving him your heart, give your yes to Jesus,
And you too will be saved.

❖ Section 7

Poems and Prose
for Black Women
& Discrimination

Why Do We Discriminate

Why do we discriminate against one another, just because of a person's skin color?
Why do you have a preconceived opinion to dislike a person for no reason and give such ill treatment?
Why all the drama, conflict and discord toward one another in and throughout the country?
The accusations of the racial and the prejudice that is being debated is causing drama and conflict among the races.
Yes we discriminate against each other and sometimes not just in color;

But in race, sex, size, religion, and each other.
Let's not forget in nationality and in politics.
Some of us are so rude and unkind and are never satisfied.
There's a complaint about everything in this world, in a world that you never even made.

We need to stop will all the complaints and the prejudice against one another,
Even in disagreeing, there is no need to cause a racial war among one another.

Stop all the judging of each other, and instead let try loving each other.
Then the next generation would be a world without so much hate and debate.

Maybe there will be equal treatment with justice and liberty for all offered on the plate.

Why do you have a preconceived opinion to dislike a person for no reason and give such ill treatment?

God is love. So why not walk in love as God would?

Why all the prejudice and why all the racism and discrimination against other people. There is no need for all the hatred just because someone is Black.

God made us like that, so if you have an issue with that
Ask God about it since he created us that way.

Everything he made is equal in his eyes and when he sees us, he doesn't look down on us for our skin color.

Look at our heart, we all came from one seed which was Adam and Eve.

From their children, from the same seed a new world began.

It was in their sin that sin entered in;
Then people changed, there was no longer true love in the world.
So why do you have a preconceived opinion to dislike a person for no reason and give such ill treatment?

Because of your preconceived opinion of someone's race and hate, you cause unfair treatment to others and treat them worse than you would your own dog or cat mate.

You pat these animals on the back with so much respect,
Yet you look at someone black without respect and turn your nose up at them.

You see some were raised that way, their parents taught them to disrespect a black person.

We all forget that the greatest commandment of the Bible is to love the Lord thy God with all thy heart and to love thy neighbor as thy self.

One day we all will be judged by the creator above, not by our color and not by our size.

Not by the amount of money we have, but by our hearts and the good that we have inside.

What is Black?

What is Black to you?
When you were born and created in the Image of God's Love.
What does Black mean to you?
When I was told that some Blacks mean nothing to them at all.
Does Black mean anything to you when some hate Black for
no reason at all?
Call us Negroes, who are ugly and dumb… Some even treat
Blacks worse than their own dog.

Why did Blacks get choose to be manipulated by those who
hate?
Why did Blacks get called uneducated, ignorant,
unknowledgeable, idiotic, dense, foolish, simpleminded and
much more than that?
You see, Black was a word that to them, meant nothing.
Why did they hate Black? Do you want to know the facts?

I believe that Black meant has more to it than being a color,
called names or the cause to be hung due to the color of a
person's skin and all.
Well I have a word to say.
God is a God of colors; if He did not want to create Black, he
would have never made us Black and that is a fact.
Why would anyone go around hating on blacks who never did
anything to them?

They were stolen from their country and made slaves. They
had no choice or else they would be dead.

Tell me this, if those people hated Blacks like that,

Then perhaps they should have taken them back.
Helpless, abused, you took advantage, for sure;
All those who hate the Blacks, I have only one thing to say
more,
If you hate the Blacks so bad,
Go ask the creator that created the Black.
Why Blacks?

I would ask the Creator, why do they hate and not like Blacks;
Perhaps the Creator may or may not be Black;
OK now, that could be a fact.
After all, we all bleed the same blood, all in all.

Phenomenal Black Women

Phenomenal Black Women, so strong and free,
Don't let things of the world blow your mind with charms,
And ONLY brilliant ideas.
There's nothing wrong with the finer things in life,
But it's about how you handle it and how to treat people right.
You see when you forget where you have come from,
You look down on people who don't have as much as you could
see.
Guess what?
Someday it might be them one day looking down at you, you
see.

A Black Mother's Pain

Do you feel the grief of a Black mother's tears?
The tears she's felt when her son is gone in a disaster caused
by a catastrophe that sudden happen, sometimes the violence
that is created can cause people lives to be gone in a second.
A mother's grief and the pain and hurt inside feel so bad, that
she doesn't know if she can survive the violence that tend to
continue with young blacks killing each other is a disgrace and
shame.

To all the Black mothers disrespected because of the color of
your skin,
Just for being Black you are destroyed by the white man.
Young Black men have to learn lessons from what has
happened to all the previous Black men who died due to the
color of their skin.

Many died before their time, because there were those that
mocked and laughed at the freedom that was had though an
person of authority, others decided not to stop the crime;
But a Black man named Martin Luther King, Jr. stood up for
Black folks one day.
He proclaimed his rights with danger in sight.

He made a point that Blacks and Whites should remember,
Walk in love, get along with each other.
Now you see you cannot forget,
What other Blacks died for and underwent,
All so that we would have rights so that the next generation
could get it right and not have to fight.

It's a shame to see Black on Black killing each other, over a things that don't matter.

The world would be a better place, if we stop the hate and just appreciate,

Appreciate all the beauty in the world and stop destroying it with this mess.

About the Author

The mission of this woman in Christ, is to strive towards complete excellence in her own life. She seeks to reach others with a positive image. She is very focused and determined to allow God to build her life to be an inspiration to others through her passionate words to be used for spiritual healing. She is a phenomenal woman with a vision and a plan and purpose to reach others with encouragement. This Collection of Prose and Poetry reaches others by Evangelizing and serving as a tool to comfort, motivate, and uplift others despite the adversity and or challenges faced in day to day living. It challenges ones thinking about themselves. Many of the items within the collection have been inspired based on the Author's own experiences.

Book Reviews

Love this book? Don't forget to leave a review! Every review matters, and it matters a *lot!* Head over to Amazon to leave an honest review for me. I thank you endlessly.

www.ingramcontent.com/pod-product-compliance
Lightning Source LLC
Chambersburg PA
CBHW072051040426
42447CB00012BB/3089